Endless River

Poems of Andrew Stephen

Endless River

Poems of Andrew Stephen

Hickathrift
Press

THE HICKATHRIFT PRESS

2024

Published by the Hickathrift Press

Text © Andrew Stephen 2024
Design © Dave Phillips 2024

First published 2024

Andrew Stephen has asserted his right
under the Copyright, Design and Patents act, 1988,
to be identified as Author of this work.

All rights reserved. Without limiting the rights under
copyright reserved above, no part of this book may be
reproduced, stored in or introduced into a retrieval
system, or transmitted, in any form, or by any
means (electronic, mechanical, photocopying,
recording or otherwise) without the written
permission of the Hickathrift Press.

Produced in England by the Hickathrift Press

DEDICATION

*To my brother Richard, who has shown
me why we should never give up*

Contents

Author's Foreword — 8

The Poems: — 15
Prologue I
Prologue II
Prologue III
Prologue IV
The Hourglass Effect
Ambition
Little Cloister
Home is Where the Heart is
Daydream
Crescat In Horas Doctrina
It's My Heritage Too
It's My Heritage Too (Reprise)
Dorset
Bridge Song
Sturminster Newton
Old Story
Meeting
May
A Little Romance
Before You
The Leap
A Taste of Melancholy
Revelation
The Actor
Shapes in the Shadows
Trainspotting

By Far the Greatest Team…
Days are for Remembering
Solitude
Peddar's Way
There Have Been Times
Out of Reach
Julia
Home
Playing Parts
Broken Dream
Is it a Race?
Lost in the Tapestry
Exile
In the City
The Hermit
Stratford
The Anniversary
Alzheimer's: a Case Study
A Rising Storm
That's Bleak
Vision
Lizzie
The Homecoming
I Think I Caught a Glimpse of Heaven
No Hiding Place
The Endless River

Endpiece	101
The Hickathrift Press	104

Foreword from the Author

"Poetry comes from the highest happiness or the deepest sorrow" — A P J Abdul Kalam

It seems extraordinary that at the age of 71 I am publishing my first anthology of poetry. It's even less likely than that, given that I abandoned or at least neglected writing poetry or much else for many years. I will tell you how it came about.

During the dark days of the covid pandemic, when we were more or less confined to barracks, I found myself wanting to explore my feelings more completely and more honestly than I had been able to do in prose. Perhaps it was a kind of therapy. I am by nature gregarious and to be kept away from social groups for such a long time was very challenging. To have the habits of a lifetime put on hold made many of us question our routines and beliefs. Poetry is the best possible vehicle for these thoughts.

If I could paint or sing or write music, I might feel differently. But I can't and I don't. Maybe that frustrated creativity feeds my poetry. It's hard to be sure. What I do know is that poetry gives me the opportunity to consider feelings that are almost beyond description. I have always believed that our lives have meaning. Even our misery usually has a purpose, although we can't always see it at the time. Losing twins when I was a young man seemed like the end of things but without that tragedy the children who followed would probably have never existed. I can't imagine that now.

When I was a student teacher in Derby, we were entertained one evening by Adrian Henri, one of the hugely successful Liverpool Beat Poets. The other act didn't turn up, so he was encouraged to keep going with the promise of unlimited wine. He stayed at our hall of residence that night and I asked him what he said to readers who interpreted lines of his poems differently. He knew the real meaning, so did he tell them that other interpretations were wrong? His reply has stayed with me. In his view, all interpretations were "correct", since meaning is made by the reader who brings their own experience to bear. In fact, as a result of hearing the opinions of his readers, he'd changed his own mind about what various lines might mean.

You can only take that view so far, because writers choose words very carefully to get across the sense of what they are trying to say, but there is a kind of freedom involved. We all see the world in different ways. We're intuitive and spiritual in our understanding of experience.

Emotion and instinct are hugely important to us all in shaping our beliefs and responses. Some feelings are almost too deep to be described and we feel our way towards what they mean. Poetry does this in a way that prose can't because prose is too literal and less evocative. Poetry reaches the parts that other writing can't. I use it to explore things I'm not quite sure of and it has helped me to appreciate some experiences more fully and deal with other feelings that have troubled me.

Poetry has also helped me to link my personality as an adolescent with that of a man in old age. I know more now, but essentially I've not really changed. I still try to see through the eyes of a child.

I became interested in poetry at school when I was about fifteen and realising that I had some aptitude for English and History and very little for anything else. We had a gifted young teacher called Dave Sim, who taught us for O Level English. He had a very glamorous American wife and a very radical disposition. He showed us that literature could be beautiful and relevant. He used song lyrics, speeches and debates to show that views were more powerful when they could be supported by well-reasoned argument. After that, I didn't mind learning and reciting bits of *Henry the Fifth*. Indeed, I can recite it now! Many years later, as a teacher, I recited part of the prologue to colleagues at the end of term. One of them cried, moved by language that had stayed with me for over forty years.

Dave Sim encouraged us to read beyond the syllabus requirements and I found that Hardy, Lawrence and the Liverpool Beat Poets had a lot to say to me. Many of us were beginning to listen to pop music, which in the Sixties was becoming increasingly sophisticated. In English lessons we studied the lyrics of Bob Dylan. I began to get the idea of evoking feelings by using association and comparison. Even then, I could see that Dylan was a genius. His voice was awful, but his lyrics were beautiful to the ear. Sixties music was about love, freedom, revolution and hippy ideals. People my age always say that music at that time was more influential than any since. Songs were agents of change. I remember listening to the whole of Sgt Pepper's Lonely Hearts Club Band being played, for the very first time, on Radio Luxembourg. I've never forgotten it. Neither have I forgotten the first time I heard the Moody Blues' *Days of Future Passed*. Even now, if I feel a bit downhearted, *Nights In White Satin* restores me.

Poetry too, can be healing, and helps me to make sense of things, whether I'm writing it and, especially, when I'm listening to it. The beauty of language has remarkable power, which is why I get so angry at the reduction of language by jargon and business speak.

Not surprisingly, I chose to do English and History, among other things, at A Level. A new English teacher, Roger Hubbard, introduced me to T S Eliot and Dylan Thomas. He made both poets intelligible to us and I have been influenced by their poetry and philosophies ever since. Quite a gift. The Welsh are known for their singing and clearly have an ear for sound. I had a number of parts in a school production of *Under Milk Wood* which, although not Dylan Thomas's greatest work, is full of words that sound like music. The sound of words carefully put together creates a meaning by itself. In a good poem, no word could possibly be replaced by an alternative.

By contrast, Eliot was an intellectual and an elitist. His poetry strained to be worthy of high culture. Roger's teaching was so good that when I later studied his poems at college, our lecturer sent me away, claiming that I understood his poetry better than she did. I don't know whether that was true or not, but I really wish I'd been able to tell him.

Back in my days as a rebellious Sixth Former, I started to write and distribute newsletters in school. Many were banned by the headmaster as "subversive". Language always is. People are only afraid of it if their own arguments are flimsy.

Roger affirmed that poetry was neither effeminate nor pointless. He also taught me how to read Shakespeare aloud and as if I meant it. I began to understand it properly then. It's certainly not just for academics. There are moments in King Lear that reduce me to tears, when an old man begins to doubt himself before reaching real self-awareness. I could never have been a scientist or to limit myself to the literal. Less idealistically, I had discovered girls – and the fact that many I met loved poetry. At first it didn't occur to me to write poems for girls I fancied, but when I did, I sometimes found it quite effective. What better motive could there be?

It amused me that some of my contemporaries avoided poetry; it seemed counter-intuitive (not that that very ugly phrase existed then). My Norfolk grammar school was for boys only and my interest was beginning to lean towards the town's high school for girls. Happily, the two schools allowed mixed meetings at both schools for members of their History and Poetry Societies. School productions also offered opportunities, as did an allegedly cultural event called Inter Sixth. By the time I left school, many of us stuffed books into our blazer pockets as a badge of honour. One girl that I was particularly fond of loved the poetry of Keats. I don't read it so much now.

During my gap year, inadvertent as it was, I worked shifts at the local canning factories and had a lot of time and money on my hands. Much of both were spent in John Prime's bookshop in King's Lynn. He sold a lot of poetry anthologies which I still have. They've survived many a cull.

I wrote a lot of poems then. Most were awful. Some got into the paper. Most were derivative, trivial or superficial. But I was learning my craft and at eighteen years old I had a lot to say. I still have them in a box file and they make me smile when I read them. They put me back in touch with a very much younger me and I like to experience all those feelings all over again fifty years later.

Sometimes it's hard to recognise our younger selves. I suspect that we become different people as we go through different phases of our lives and face different challenges but in some ways we don't change at all. I still have a lot to say. I like to review what I have experienced and try to approach things in different ways; I get excited when I'm doing something new. Writing poetry has helped to unify my experiences and keep me young at heart. At least I think so.

A lot of the poems I wrote as a teenager were about the illusions of young love, the pain of rejection, idealism about the future and the search for meaning. My early experiences of work and mixing with adults weren't very inspiring and writing was a means of escape. It led me to thinking about college and teaching. My former teachers Ken Gregory and Roger Hubbard set me up with interviews and encouraged me to take my poetry with me. My poems formed part of my interview for teachers' training college in Derby and, a few months later, I became a student.

Before I began, I finished a batch of poems inspired by hitchhiking to the West Country. Some of my dissolute ancestry came from Bridport in Dorset and the novels and poetry of Thomas Hardy had inspired me to believe in the old magic of Wessex and all the evidence of ancient peoples to be found there. I was a Romantic and I was in love – or thought I was. First love is never forgotten and being spurned for the first time is never forgotten either. She of the predilection for Keats and a vaguely spiritual belief in St Agnes Eve was always intended for me.

Anyway, I hitched down to Dorset to meet this remarkable young lady on the bridge at Sturminster Newton. Standing there, holding her hand, I realised that it had all been a delicious delusion. Tragically, she was killed in a road accident when she was only twenty-one. I still visit her grave in East Winch churchyard, almost opposite where she lived. I have been back to Sturminster since, but the dream is long gone. The poems are all I have of her. Perhaps it is all we ever have.

In Derby I carried on writing and the principal's wife took a lot of interest in me and in my writing. She knew poets and people who published with the Arvon Press. For a time I imagined that they might publish me, but I didn't really believe in myself enough to pursue it. My scribblings ended up in a box where they yellowed and were forgotten for decades. Marriage, teaching, children, homemaking and real life replaced dreams and poetry. Not that I'm complaining. Without the experiences of real life there can be no poetry – none of value anyway.

Well into my career as a teacher I began to write newsletters, originally as bulletins for my staff. These expanded to a point where I began to write on a number of topics. By the time I left teaching, the *Bulletin*, or *Sentinel* as it was then named, was distributed to the entire staff on a Friday afternoon. The name had to be changed because the headmaster banned the *Bulletin*. Déjà vu. In retirement the *Bulletin* became the *Phoenix* and I experimented with many writing styles. I began to write autobiographical fragments and the odd poem. I loved the freedom of verses, where imagination and emotion once again led me to ideas I thought I'd left behind.

The box file was found again and I reworked some of the pieces about my old grammar school for the former pupils' newsletter, *The Lennensian*. I am an Old Lennensian and now the editor of that august publication. As I revisited that old material I found, unexpectedly, that new poems were coming to me – poems that explored the passing of time, the landscape, inherited memory and the relationship between youth and old age.

During the pandemic the search for meaning became more insistent. Life is a short and brittle thing and I wanted to explore the idea that there was some purpose to it all. Increasingly I felt that relationships, friendships, family and what we contribute to other peoples' lives are the things that matter most. I think that my later poems show this. I hope they do.

My final poem, *The Endless River,* supplies the title for this anthology. It combines my memories of the River Ouse as it passes through King's Lynn with my own voyage through the challenges of youth to the alleged wisdom of old age. The view of the river was familiar to me during my formative years and I see it often now that I have moved back to Norfolk. It's the place I love best, full as it is of beautiful old churches where the very stones remember all the generations that have tried to imagine concepts far greater than individuals.

You can't really express the idea with precision, any more than you can describe the sound of rooks at sunset, or the sunlight filtering through the cries of the lonely sounds of seabirds in the salt marsh. I have tried though and poetry is the only means I have to express who I am and all that I've known. The Endless River still flows. I hope you enjoy my efforts to show you why.

Andrew Stephen
Norfolk, May 2024

The Poems

The Prologue series of four poems that follow were written many years after the feelings described within them had passed.

There's no pain quite like the first time the person you thought adored you and thought you perfect dumps you in favour of someone else. It doesn't seem possible and it throws all kinds of beliefs and perceptions into doubt. Of course the feeling is temporary but never forgotten. These poems show how I tried to make sense of what had happened and my attempts to be positive and move on.

Years later I learned how to forgive and to realise that no one is our property and that no feeling lasts for ever. It is a privilege to connect with someone, even if it causes pain. I now realise that anyone ending a relationship suffers a bit, even if they were in the driving seat. Wisdom is expensive to acquire though.

Prologue 1

My eyes are closing
To the music of my mind.
All seems past
As, half aware,
I feel those times
And search for the songs
Which amused us both
As we listened to the words
Which were all about us.

I imagine her now
In some dusty and dimly-lit room
Intently hunched over her table
Much as she used to
Thinking about lines of careless chatter
And measured remarks.

The wind removes my footsteps
And friendly voices have forgotten my name.
All seems familiar,
She turns
And looks into the dark unknown
Which we feared in our smug
Forgetfulness.

The wind removes my footsteps
And friendly voices have forgotten my name.
All seems familiar,
Is there an empty chair? A silent space that speaks for me?
Rain, remorseless and wicked winds whip
The dead days passing.
The dawn is coming
But her thoughts lack form
Or power
In that room
Where echoes drown my memory.

Prologue II

And so silence speaks to me
Since your old truths
Cannot be found
Or heard
In my head or in the memory of your face
Quizzical, still and secret now.

Once your thoughts met mine
And wandered, liberated,
Along indifferent miles.
It seems so long ago,
And my eyes strain
To glimpse
What used to be so clear.

It seems that I know
Nothing of you now.
My instincts played me false
And I doubt my own pointless grief.
We always think we know
Where our intended path leads
It seems that my past was misconceived
And so
My smile forgets with satisfaction
The days that never were.

"My eyes strain to glimpse what used to be so clear"

Prologue III

Talking thus to myself
Makes things seem deliberate
And yet my new silence
Is not forgetful.
You have chosen
A world which is not mine
Summer without joy
Waters without reflection
Music without sound
Wealth without content.
Your liberation is mine to share,
Your thirst
For a better offer
Unquenchable.
My lesson will be less bitter
Than yours.
My memories
Will be mine.

"You can never grow old in my dreams"

Prologue IV

Your anger once amazed me
The doubling back
On a wrong choice
Which suddenly seemed absurd
A kind of doom
A darkness
Where no one wants to look.
I hesitated
My thoughts
Like an aching tooth
Never went away.

You can never grow old
In my dreams
Your promise will never end
Because it never truly began.
I fall
As I must
But I cling to life
As one who will not be drowned
By your destruction.

The Hourglass Effect suggests that striving too hard makes it difficult for us to find our own way or even to know what that is. It was influenced by my reading of Hermann Hesse, who believed that the answers to the most intractable problems lie within. We just have to let them emerge. I read Damian when I was in the sixth form. I've been reading Hesse ever since. I might have been a Buddhist. I was a bit too young to be a hippy.

"Success measures itself with smiles we don't need to make"

The Hourglass Effect

Stand here with the flute I borrowed
Can't play a note
Stand by the water's edge
Only watching
As the tides change
Waiting for the tomorrow
I know must arrive.

Money spending in a bar
Voice changing as the evening drags out
Sad
At wasting effort
And the clock's moving into the night
With the times I haven't found.
What you see and what you hear
Mock any wish
To be different
To be seen.

Somewhere there is a voice unhurried
Gentle and calm
Not cracked and dry
Like paint on the ceiling
Or brash and pointless posturing.
We find our own words
Without chasing them
And our own way
Without striving.
Success
Measures itself
With smiles
We don't need to make.

This poem is about someone I knew who died when she was very young. The fear of youth and our desire to grow up too soon is a theme which has preoccupied me at times. We can't know what we might become or how long we've got. Freedom is knowing that there is never just one way or one destination.

Ambition

So it was there
Observed by those same trees
You dwelt among book and aspiration
Shining, a schoolgirl
Biking past orchids
Asleep like the canal
And sharing with the fields
Thoughts too soon
For your smiling face.
Ah, your hair blew free in the wind
But your fear of youth
Was too much like your cold room
With its wall white
And relentless clock.

"You dwelt among book and aspiration: shining, a schoolgirl"

ENDLESS RIVER 23

I remember very well the day I first set eyes on the Little Cloister. I had been to London with my A Level Economics and Public Affairs group. Barry King, our trendy, young, lefty teacher had arranged for us to meet Derek Page, our MP, after a tour of the House of Commons. He didn't show up, so we didn't get to climb Big Ben. But we did meet Liberal leader Joe Grimmond at the Underground station and we went to Westminster Abbey, which was free admission and much more accessible than it is now. We touched the Stone of Scone and sat in the Confessor's throne.

Eventually we ended up in the part of the abbey which is still monastic. I stood looking at the fountain and listening to its subtle sounds, aware that the hurly-burly of the capital was just yards away.

It's an image I still have in my head when times are tough. I've shown the fountain to a number of people but my feelings about it can't be described. It still seems a miracle that such a simple thing could have so much power.

I wrote this poem many years ago after I'd stumbled upon this place. I returned to it quite recently. Amazingly, those feelings returned.

> *"Gazing into the random spray of a perfect fountain I felt the touch of Eternity"*

Little Cloister

Through a timeless arch
It seemed that I had escaped
From the modern rush and noise
Into a place of peaceful past.
I had not wished for
Any of this
Sense of holiness and safety
A moment separated
From where I was going.
I saw
Perfection in solid stone
Made wonderful by the patience of time.
Mystical forgetfulness
Brought a new way of knowing
A few minutes only
This time of revelation
But
Gazing into the random spray
Of a perfect fountain
I felt the touch of Eternity.

"The churches belong here, sunk by time into slight hillsides"

Home is Where the Heart is

There blows a cold east wind
Which is hardly less than rain
Rooks above the sodden fields
Give raucous comment
As the forgotten ponds
And gleaming flints ache to be painted
Beneath impossible skies
Vast and permanent.
The churches belong here
Sunk by time into slight hillsides
Moulded by weather
And ignored by gangs of hares
Stupidly unafraid and skittish
Familiar as the smell of beet
And woodsmoke on autumn nights.

We are always close to water
And to an ancient past
Which we cherish.
Our lives are just another turn in the road
In the minutes before the sun goes down
And the massive trees
Slowly disappear
From our contented eyes.

"Light dies naturally, leaving amplified memories in the uncertain night when only the mind speaks"

Daydream

Limp hands loosely grip a caring past
Shadows of what they were
Amongst an endless sand,
Reflections of hope bravely bright
With the slow sea following
And whispering an old truth.

Light dies naturally
Leaving amplified memories
In the uncertain night
When only the mind speaks.
Recollections of the first kiss
As the sun sank
Too slowly to see.

More than half a century ago, in the glowing embers of a summer's day, a boy at the King Edward VII Grammar School in King's Lynn, Norfolk, was so captivated by the glow of the school's red brickwork in the sunset he was moved to poetry.

That boy was me. I hope my poem is as appropriate today as it was back in 1970, when Mungo Jerry's In The Summertime topped the pop charts.

PS: Crescat In Horas Doctrina is the school motto. It means "Let him hourly increase in learning"

Crescat In Horas Doctrina

I stumble across you
Basking in sympathetic dusk
Unexpected and beautiful
Solitary, strong and precise
Definite against the dark's subtle encroachment
Flattering the ambition
Of some painter's gaudy sunset
With lines
Far too sombre for me.
Familiarity fades
With the moody fancy
And the calm dignity
Of a forgotten creator's vision
Returns to my unsuspecting eyes.
I share the moment
With my past
In silence.
If I dare to turn my back
Will I understand
Any of this
Ever again?

It's My Heritage Too

Here, in a scholar's dusty palace,
Given leave to think my own thoughts,
I am listening to another generation's pride
Between the fact barrage and instinctive denial.
We, the unappreciative
Are both slack
And exact
In our differences.
And wasn't it always
Chalk and chairs
And longing for a better past?
Preservation seems like a King
Of Death
Based on a lie
And the security of habit.

Sitting in this too-sober silence
Chatter mounts in my head
As our betters try,
Yet again,
To impose their youth
On us
Like some sort of favour.
A beginning of sorts
Is waiting for us,
A deliverance from
The endlessly sly
Character tests
Imposed on us
For our own good.

This fear of change
Calls itself
Authority
And sneers
At the inevitable.

"Wasn't it always chalk and chairs and longing for a better past?"

It's My Heritage Too (Reprise)

There now the cave of hope and experience
Has burst open
I am hearing another generation's certainty
Those familiar crimson walls
Have mellowed with nostalgia
We are wiser
Or older
The shadows of our youth
Lurk along those corridors
Strangely smaller, shorter
And . . .

The revolution came and went
Along with our hair
Woodstock, Vietnam and the howls of protest
Dreams which we thought were ours alone
We are only a career away
Like our masters
Who saw Spitfires and the Raj
As their memories
The twinkling of an eye
Has created History
As it always must.

All that forgotten anger
And long lessons learned
Led to trying a better way
To bring children a glimpse
Of independence and ambition
My pupils
Imposed their youth on me
As they found their voice

Their hopes and joy
Were a gift to me
And all the answer
To my quest.

"The shadows of our youth lurk along those corridors"

Dorset

Something summons my rambling soul
A voice I must answer
The wind, a sigh,
I must look for a reason
Some ancient purpose.
Trees sweetly sleep
Where rivers crawl calling
And life knows not nor wants, future.
Here nothing has, or can, change,
Such security draws me on.
Love itself was formed here
Where nothing competes
In hazy, never-ceasing afternoons
And timeless churches,
Here, where love's futures framed
Inspirations as reliable as the churning seasons
And thus, Destiny calls me,
Has called me, in the way of
Time's trick of perpetual existence
To seek myself.

"The rays of the sun strike gentle on the riverside"

The Bridge Song

The weary day breaks
With tired eyes
Watching the vague shapes clamour
As the world begins to make its money,
And, by the perpetual bridge,
The rays of the sun
Strike gentle
On the riverside
Where once, for a time,
Time was forgotten.

I could never ignore
Such smiles as changed that world
Can't imagine the ache before conclusion
When it was good just to live,
And better – I recall.
When the long day found me waiting
No hurrying midst a mindless flight
I heard countless tunes of the air
Each more beautiful than the last.
They harmonise in the river's glitter-gaze
In an infinitely moving moment
Long as a sigh
And safe as an embrace.

Sturminster Newton

Sturminster still I see
Sun filled, blank eyed, smiling, end of the journey
As I crossed the long-imagined bridge
And remembered the beginnings.
The miles wind in memory
Waiting, satisfied, as the slow river
Introduced me, using more than words
To a world that wasn't mine to remember.
I had been shown
From early days
An unfathomed secret,
Mine for time's destruction.
She, sad in solitary recollection.

Too cruel this eye-opening,
Unending riddle of time and journeys
Along new roads
Leading to new ways,
An untold story
Waiting to be heard,
Waiting to be understood.

This moment
Was always waiting,
An appointed hour
Where roads met
Before diverging
To search for a new destiny.

"This moment was always waiting"

When I wrote Sturminster Newton, I had been reading Tennyson. I've been influenced by his poem Ulysses all my life. I understand that there will always be another adventure until one day there isn't. When my son took me to New York, I had never expected to be there and loved it. Life should be an adventure and old men ought to be explorers.

This poem is a bitter one which tries not to be. Human emotions are often contradictory and sometimes we refuse to see what we know to be true. I began this poem in 1971 and didn't complete it until 2022.

Old Story

With sudden assurance
Came new life,
She, cruelly penitent
Had apologised.

Evasive joy
Obscures the flashing danger signals
Pushed out of sight
Wilfully,
Knowingly.
Knowledge in the hands
Of desperate desire
Is as brittle as a heart
Filled with hope
And delusion.

So, read on,
With deeply transient wisdom
The words of rejection.
The letter,
Painfully unique
Soon they join the pile of words
That didn't work.

Meeting

I see the eyes which do not look
Hear the whirling words
Which go nowhere
The high-minded experts
Who judge and decide
Promoting their virtue
While one thinks alone

Look at the blatant ambition
The platforms of vanity
Those intricate niceties
Which simulate taste.
Social success is strenuous
Critics accuse with acquired venom
While he who stands alone smiles
Free.

"As brittle as a heart filled with hope and delusion"

May

And so we find another May
New in repeated blossom
And warm-glow seasoned sun.
The day moves gentle
Like long-forgotten hints of breezes
And slower
Than those who sit in silence
Outwitting the impatient ones
With too much to perform.
Reaching its final drawn-out hours
Some are granted
Its wonder blessing
Of calm evening.
Careless smiles and excited voices
Mark the timeless grassy freedom
And find us remembering forgotten summers
And lonely gardens by rivers
Which twist through our dreams.
Worried and unhurried
Sharpened by solitude
Destiny lurks elusive
Whether leaves waste away
Or the sleeping sad
Is stirred by the promise
Of seasons yet to come.

A Little Romance

Once I saw my medieval lady
Hiding in the leaves
Blown, wet like the wind,
Her voice, stringed and silky
The music of the trees.

Her eyes were like a joyful morning
Her skin patterned with sunlight
And her music, which was silent
Echoed sometimes.

I sit sad with knowledge
Framing my words
In an open white sky
Sensing willow and pipe
Garden and song
But the lady who smiled has returned
Inside.

Before You is a new poem about feelings I had many years ago. Sometimes when I write, feelings I thought long forgotten return to me very powerfully. I became aware of girls and the way relationships, however fleeting, transform our view of the world.

Having felt anger, bitterness and disappointment in stages, I am old enough now to be profoundly grateful for the ways in which my rather stale perceptions were challenged and enriched. Love is a wonderful thing.

Before You

Before you
Days were just days
And my jagged words
Would never fit together.
Before you
The colours of Summer
Were just grass and trees and shadows
Waiting for laughter
To bring them to life.

Before you
Old films were just Autumn
Black and white departures
With dead leaves scurrying across tragic scenes
The river sinking
In a mortuary of brown
And pointless beauty.

Before you
The park stood empty
And neglected,
The old walls were just a reminder of other people's lives
This town's secrets were confused
And hidden.

I won't forget
How the language of smiles
Brought my world to life
And how I never saw it
Before you.

We rarely thank the people who bring something to our lives. I was in conversation with someone the other day and he mentioned the name of a former girlfriend. Then this happened...

The Leap

Strange how a gesture
Can reach through time itself,
A name, a story, a smile
Lighting up
Moments hidden from view
In a future
Never imagined.

The guilt of neglect
Sometimes lies heavy on me
I never learned
To stride out alone
Without your clear-sighted confidence.

We are foolish to believe
That anything we make
Is ours alone
Or that no one really sees us.
We never get the chance
To show the regret
Learned from years of toil
And hankering for rest.
You sensed my secret world
Long before I did
And I never told you
That now I trust my instinct
And see in perfect colour
That you showed me how.

"You sensed my secret world long before I did"

"Our endless walks where life bubbled with joy"

This poem is about the relationships that might have lasted if circumstances or real life hadn't got in the way. I sometimes wonder what happened to the people I knew as a young man. I have been fortunate enough to meet a number of them in recent years and again it suggests that there has been some purpose to it all. Comparing notes about times long past makes them a little more real, although that dream-like quality remains too. We are all entitled to our illusions.

A Taste of Melancholy

Do you think of me now
When the dark drags me away?
Mournful choirs, the tragic organ notes echoing
in ruins.
Neglected graveyards are what I see.
Yet this is dissatisfaction
Of the deep, intense, loving kind
The wind whispers your name
And the trees laugh no longer
But seem to sigh my contentment
All those different notes
Now seem in harmony
Our endless walks
Where life bubbled with joy
In the dappled afternoon sun
Or dozed contentment
In the gentle rain
Of comfort.
And so,
I will be on my way again
Ready to return
Travelling dream struck
Into our night.

Revelation

It seems to me
That the world smiles
Sometimes
Like it's allowing me
To join in the joke
And, just as the so-dramatic sigh
Tries to do justice to knowing,
The nervous fiddling
Ceases and finds its expected reward
That strange, animal throb
Greeting the special moments
We were only waiting to treasure,
Hidden, in some frantic city street
Bored, tired and mechanical,
Where speech stretches
To mean something,
The stream of cigarettes
Always ending
In disappointed mouths
And lit by old hopes
Searching for mystery
The ecstasy of the unknown.
The floating castles of dreams
Fade with the light
And the dullness of mechanical
Leisure
Until your face
Offers me a vision
Which
Old words can't describe.

*"Your face offers
me a vision
old words
can't describe"*

The Actor

We all need a moment longer
To delay the swaying curtain
Soon to reveal our frailties
And expose the hidden gaps.
There is a moment
Of suspended silence
Before, gladiator-like,
We turn to face our judges.

Our voices surprise us
Loud and lonely
In the suddenly disturbed stillness
Rehearsed, mechanical
But somehow untamed.
Soon we become ourselves
Or one of them
Competing with our shadows
Suddenly dancing in our prisons.
Their eyes erase our doubts
As each test fades into memory.

We only want to be invisible
But to perform is to live.

"Their eyes erase our doubts"

Shapes in the Shadows

All those years
I was waiting for the door to slam
Shut on lonely dreams
The silence which once filled my head
Is groping towards words to still the ache
Of endless energy
And restless searching
For meaning
And something more
Than mere memory
Which burns on
Like a solitary bulb
Revealing only part
Of our separateness.

We imagine our irrelevance
Hide in the fog
And noise
Of uncertainty,
Not sure about promises made
Pictures seen
Or words which
Expose us.
Sad whistles
Echo outside.
The slow-moving river
Is whipped by the wind.
Cold feet tramp
Along wet pavements
As we are called to consciousness.

Each moment is precious
Each hurt worthwhile
Your spirit hangs still in the air
Your promises have brought me life.

ENDLESS RIVER 55

"Your spirit hangs still in the air"

Trainspotting

They tell me
That it's the smell
Of oil and steam
Or the haunting whistle
Slowly fading into
Its solitary emptiness.
It is that characteristic hiss
Or rhythmic drumming
Of huge machines
Made human by sentiment
And our childhood dreams.

I love all that
And the Victorian pride
In architecture
Made to impress
And made special
Through familiarity
And the pride
Of generations.

But it isn't that.
It's always been
The sadness of departure
And separation.
It is the thrill
Of anticipation
Arrival and reunion
The passing vistas.

And the strangers
We know for a while.

All our lives long
We are travelling
Looking for the happiness we lost
And the sweet promise
Of tomorrow.

"We are looking for the happiness we lost and the sweet promise of tomorrow"

By Far the Greatest Team

Across the misty allotments
Where men escape
And smoke and mutter,
Through the faded curtains
Of my nana's bedroom,
Gleam the great and yellow lights
Majestic in the dark nights
Shining on the theatre
Of our passing dreams.

Bovril and tea
Old men in macs
With pipes
And reluctant opinions
Surround the pitch
As expectations rise
With the crowds
As success builds on success
And little Cambridge
Startle the giants.

As a boy
I knew only dimly
About closed shops and jobs for the boys.
Bradford Park Avenue
Sounded exclusive to me
All those years ago.

We have been to Wembley
Beaten the richest club on Earth
On their own turf
Overcome decline
And near-extinction
To thrill generations

Year after year
Bringing our children
And grandchildren
To touch their heritage
And feel the anguish and the joy.

Your club chooses you
I say
As once it chose me.
It's in our blood
And inherited by right.
Be proud.

"Gleam the great and yellow lights, majestic in the dark nights"

Days are for Remembering

This finger of shafted sun
Pokes the drowsy dust of dead night
And stirs the early morning visions,
Dreams and fantasies
Of the retreats and escapes
Of the new-pounding mind.

So begins a complex circuit
In amongst the intricate morning thoughts,
The memos and satisfactory conclusions
And the careless afternoon's dozing
And Sunday sunbeams shine.

With such unhurried drift
A peaceful blend of Nature's voices
Not least yours
Circles my dreams
As I lay, undisturbed.

"This finger of shafted sun stirs early morning visions"

Solitude

Sitting alone by a fresh-painted window
Granted time to think
Of the perfect beauty
Of sliding raindrops on rooftops
Ripples on shining streams
Lines of light
On a distant horizon.

Alone
Without a thought
Except the blurring of light
Secure
Protected in peace
By a shield of glass.

A bonfire in the distance
Smoulders its slow death.
A flat-capped man,
Indispensible, integral
Digs deep into the fresh earth.

An untroubled mind is a wonder
Freedom is all we need
And eyes to see.
How beautiful it is
To be alone.

Peddars Way

Our paths lead back
To many stories which we cannot know or see
But, rather, feel, like the mist curling from the dewy ground
As we amble past ancient tumuli
On our way to the sea.
Confined to our own fanciful thoughts
We are like hermits
With the heart of a good friend hidden inside
A mystery to everyone
But ourselves.
All my words have lived inside me
Struggling to get out and rhyme with someone else's without being spoken
Our thoughts search for homes
Where all is acceptance
All understood
Where a glance is like music
And time means nothing
In your eyes.

"All my words have lived inside me, struggling to get out and rhyme with someone"

There Have Been Times

There have been times
When I wondered
Why I ignored
The promise
Which echoed in your words and
Wicked eyes.

Times when
I thought that your heart
Could be unlocked
And bring me to myself.
The surging tides
And fleeting moments
Which terrified me
With unprovoked joy.

There have been times
When I wondered where you were
And why you are not with me
Sharing my uncertainty
Riding the wave
Blinking in the sunshine
And walking through the trees.

There are times
When I thought
That was the moment
You brought me to myself
And you never left.

Out of Reach

Memory, like a shaft of sunlight
Seems almost real
In the swirl of dusty realisation
And barely understood instincts.
It shines on the face
And in the eyes
Dizzy with
The dangerous fruit of longing.
This gnarled corner
Of my mind
Is choked with desires and dreams
Where sweat and chatter
Meets the vision of the child
Who sees his own inevitable sorrow
In an instant
And moves on to the next game.

Julia

Your eyes reflected in mine
Already know what I know.
Inside your gaze
Is yesterday and tomorrow
Unforeseen or imagined
And yet, meant to be.
A miracle of chance
A stone tape
Recorded before the moment itself.

I was always a child too
Ignorant in my hopes and
Blind desires,
Spinning recklessly
In rage and disconnected futility,
Searching for the purpose
That was always there.

I always knew your face
Felt the difference
You were born to make.
You don't have my look
Or my learned limits
But I am part of you
And you
Will always be my liberation
From drifting, lonely
Inside my own storm.

"You will always be my liberation"

Home

This so-familiar soil
Is sucked in sodden abandon
Beneath my restless feet
All seemed as it had before
When I would glow triumphant
After my easy
And thoughtful, mystical run.
Simple paths through the trees
Uncluttered by ambition
Or intellect.

What magic spell
Could match this eastern mist?
What silent wisdom
Was ever of this inherited kind?
I see long-forgotten faces
Which followed their own paths
But left a trace of their lives
In all the seasons since.

This town
Which bred our hopes and strengths
Echoes with their footsteps
And ready smiles
From ancient ruins to coffee bars
From the square
To the station
The insistent voices
Of those who long to return
And who never really left.

"This town bred our hopes and strengths"

72 ENDLESS RIVER

This poem was inspired by a lingering memory of my fear as a teenager before the opening night of Reluctant Heros, a school play. It also relates to the insecurity we all feel.
All teachers are actors and fear being found out. Sometimes, and quite unexpectedly, I suffer a fear of public speaking. No idea why. I've always done it. So the poem is a bit of a confession I suppose.

"No one sees the nightmares locked behind the mask"

Playing Parts

I always wondered
Whose voice that was
Posturing, worrying
Waiting for the curtain to open
As the audience
With hungry eyes
Waits to devour
The gladiator, the performer
The creator of visions
Judges
In my own mind's court.
Whose voice is that
Loud and distant which sounds like mine?
In time it will return
And rejoice in
Playing to the gallery,
Fuelled by fear
And delight.

We are never quite found out
No one knows our doubts
And fragility
No one sees all of our face
Or the nightmares
Locked securely behind the mask.
As each scene ends
The thrill of survival fades
We strut and fret for a while
And never regain
The moments
Which measure
Who we are.

Broken Dream

Sleepless night's quick breath dreams
Slowly distort and reform,
Images of former times
And forgotten thoughts
Still insisting, the day's swirls and whirls
Of answerless questions
That cannot be ignored
Or brought to book.

Such prolonged self-provoked agony
Cannot be changed,
For all this elusively hopeful disdain.
Nothing changes pain's determined
Intervention,
Whilst all else ebbs and recedes
With seductive slowness.

Love flickers
And disappears,
Like the lit and flickering lanterns
Of wanton optimism
My foolish desire
For security
Saddens me.

Time awaits my waiting
Ravenous and corrosive
The doubts which swim
In among the lost joys
Where joy and sympathy
Look at each other
With little recognition.

"Joy and sympathy look at each other with little recognition"

They say
That love is eternal
Trustworthy
Honest
But my Wonder's wonder
Is forgotten
As the moment fades
Like me
In her careless mind.

Is it a Race?

It isn't a sequence
It isn't a dream
But disconnected images
Which fall like cards, helpless to the ground.
I remember the ambitions
Which throbbed like angry music
When every face was a challenge
And every bar offered hope.

There seemed to be no end
To the days of work
And scrutiny,
No limit to where we might get to
Or time to reach the top,
An endless sea of changing faces
With clever things to say.
The ambitions changed shape
And revealed themselves as grinning imposters
As children took their place
And soothed the endless yearning
The relentless search for meaning
Or fame.

I never meant to be old
Or to have so much to remember,
Didn't think that it would pass so quickly
Or look so strange
In the mirror of time.
I wonder if I am wise
Or, simply, very slow
Appearing thoughtful, true.

We never know
Quite what we are
What we can do
Or what we mean.
We must carry on exploring
Until there no seas left to sail.

"I never meant to be old or have so much to remember"

78 ENDLESS RIVER

"We grow best when we look outside"

Lost in the Tapestry

Others have left things behind
And wandered aimlessly
In the dark and hidden inside
We tread our thoughts
Into the road of purpose,
A long street
Where we breathe philosophy
Into the leaves. We flee from the flimsy embrace
Of understanding
And attachment,
Scared of loss
And frightened of being wanted.

We are different, unique
But the jealous gift of friendship
Is something we must be brave enough
To deserve.
Our possessions are ungained
Our treasure unsought.
We dance in the eyes of others
And grow best
When we look outside.

Exile is about my time as a student in Derby in the 1970s. I realised that I missed Norfolk and its ways. In King's Lynn people would remember your name and strangers would speak. It seemed quite impersonal in a big, industrial city.

I felt a mixture of curiosity about a different way of living but also some frustration at obvious shortcomings in the lifestyle I became part of. I was disappointed that college life wasn't wildly exciting or challenging.

Many of my friends left Norfolk in a restless desire to see the world. Many moved back. Derby felt like a place with an interesting past but not much future. Perhaps it was just the way I was feeling.

Exile

Here there are no
Ancient Stones
Or apple song
From the West
Or Cornish spray
Which echoes the pirate voice
And jealous celebration
Of the authentic.

No Northern
Natural acceptance
Or friendly recognition
Boasting of traditions
Where men are turned out
Like pastry
By their strong and possessive
Women.

Down South
They speak well
And rejoice in books
And boats
And suburban religions.

Here, in this alien town,
Ambition has carried me beyond my hopes.
The hope once glimpsed
Through woodsmoke
Now hidden by my blind intentions.

Too many people
So much rush
Most of what I know
Is wordless
Silent and bound up in the seasons
And the gentle rain.

As I sleep
I walk the rivers
And quiet country tracks
Amongst the craggy trees and raucous rooks.
I hear the voices
Of those who long to return
And who never really left.

> Like the previous poem (Exile), this one reflects on city life. In our rush to achieve and compete we seem to lose patience with all the good things which are already in us. Many of us rushed out of Lynn to the big city and the big time. I don't regret it, but I'm glad I'm home now!

In the City

We all wanted to know
What it was like
In the bright lights
Where whims and fads
Become rules
And looking the same
Becomes remarkable.

Here
No one has a name
We are not recognised in the street
As we rush
To get ahead
Shout
To be heard
And blend in to be different.

And so
A lifetime passes
In a haze
As we try to succeed
Without knowing why.
We work, we marry,
We do our bit
And forget nothing
Except ourselves.

"We all wanted to know what was it like in the bright lights"

This was a tough poem to write. It's about how we blame people for not fitting into the way we see things and allow friendships that we should cling to just disappear.

The Hermit is a confessional. We often hide our true selves and don't recognise the debt we owe to those who see through the mask. The most significant people in our lives help us to see ourselves. Usually, they have no realisation of our gratitude or the effect they have on our lives. There are a number of people I wish I could have thanked. As a youngster my gratitude seemed like a luxury.

"The face of the Hermit often hides a true friend's heart"

The Hermit

I have found
Though it took too long
That the face of the Hermit
Often hides
A true friend's heart.
Sometimes I saw
Those who left me behind.
They weren't laughing
But sad as the singer
Whose song is always a solo
And whose words
Fall short.

So many stories
Remain untold, unsaid and unknown
Because the terror
Of showing ourselves
Grows
With the efforts we make.

Forgive me
For not seeing
What you were
And what you brought.
The greatest wonders
Are free and unforced
And I wish
That I could lay your head on my shoulder
And take your cares away.

This poem is about how places remember and how much we learn in places of significance. This sort of feeling is particularly strong when we come back again and again.
I remember in a film version of Cider With Rosie, Laurie Lee meets his younger self coming down a country lane. I identified with that.
Places do it; so do music, smells and writing. When I've had some sense of what my younger self, things fall into place. Nothing is random or pointless.

Stratford

Strange that on a still Stratford afternoon
The sky should wander
Unimpeded across my careless gaze
Much as it should
When water stirred lilies spin
In the darkly bubbling stream
In our green English fields
Determined to be looked at.
Warm Cotswold stone
Calms the frantic tourist shrieks
And memories of other roses
And the dank earth
Curl tantalising
Away from our eyes.

This familiar town
Settles in thoughts of times forgotten
And the mists of words that strain
To capture moments
Which flow like smoke
While brutal sounds of the present
Clatter amongst the dreams
And a million photographs
Revert to daub and wattle.

The Anniversary

Faces stare back
Across the years
Silent accusations
Of what we became
And of what might have been.
Old photos, out of focus,
Blurred and vague
Echo hints of fifty years fewer
Of striving, changing and searching,
Never realising
That there is no path.

Those I might have loved
Or known properly
Have moved on
From those moments
Where all seemed possible.

Paused for a moment
The headlong rush to be grown up
And fears carefully hidden
From each other and from ourselves.

I did not belong in those pictures
And those searing moments
Only touched me for a while but they still haunt
The attic of my mind.

"Those moments where all seemed possible"

The title of this poem is deeply ironic because sufferers from this cruel disease are people and not merely cases. It's about my mother, who made a significant contribution to her community.

Social care is a mess and it's terrible that I have to remind various authorities that a woman of 92 needs and deserves care. As a society we don't look after our old people in the way former generations did. It is to our eternal shame. It's a difficult thing to write about or to understand but no civilised society can behave as we do and hold its head high.

Alzheimer's – a Case Study

You launched me into Romsey
After a long and painful struggle
Against Ignorance and fear.
I resisted my birth
As you caught glimpses
Of the insistent smoke
Swirling upwards
From the giant chimney
Of the Incinerator.

You struggled against rumour
And speculation
As Dad embarked for Suez
To save our Empire
And thwart the Insurgents
We followed him
Down the years
Around the counties
Along the Rhine
And in the shadows of Aphrodite.

Then Home called you back
And the career you longed for
And I wrote your essays

As you trained
To run Barnwell's Library
And to make
All those you got to know
Feel welcome.

Old and young
Became your friends
You read to children
Led by example
Transporting us with stories
And treasuring the memories of the old.

Time is slow now
The neighbours you remember
Have gone from you.
Your mind is muddled
And won't do what you need
It comes and goes and betrays you
Like your elusive memory.
Every decision needed
Brings a new terror
Which won't go away.

Our pocket battleship
Craves company and care
Where are the friends and dignity
You deserve?

Your mask drops
From your face in repose
Blank and somehow absent
But I know that you are still there
When you smile with your eyes
And clutch me to you
More tightly than ever.

A Rising Storm

If the Gates of Time
Would open to an impulse
From a song,
Perhaps
The music of your mind would turn to me
And the days that grind
Into the next
Might turn to summer's plea.

Times lost, times gone,
That care is surely past.
The time that came for us
And then
Was surely meant to last?

As the rain slaps dismal
On the sodden fields outside,
Only a madman would laugh.
And yet I smiled
As something which gnawed
At my restless mind
Was washed away,
Bringing rest
To the loaded hours
Bloodshot
With too much concern
And too much damning testimony.
We wait for the explosion
And yet
We find ourselves again
And accept
What comes.

That's Bleak

Onion wrapped
And mapped like a palm
My mind is cast like a net
Wide like a Norfolk sky
Black like the earth
And blown with portents
And pasts born like leaves.
Among the stone porches' drip
And stump which singing sits
Beneath the rainbow smile
And splits the sky's
Limits of horizon
And lowering cloud.
We wait and wonder
As the fierce winds
Tear our loves to pieces.

Foggy and grey
Fresh and vital
The sun's motion
Frames the frozen fields.
Ice and furrow slope
Dimly remembering
As we peer into the past
And find ourselves
Right here.

Lizzie

I little thought
When angry, angular, awkward and making my way
In a widening world
Crazed with agitation
And unspoken dreams,
That your loving face
Would still be smiling
So clearly and so kindly
Now that I am Home.

This place
Which I always loved
Has welcomed me
And accepted me again,
Now much older, calmer
But never wiser.
I never knew
What your love
Meant to me
Or how your laughter
Would be my tune
For always.

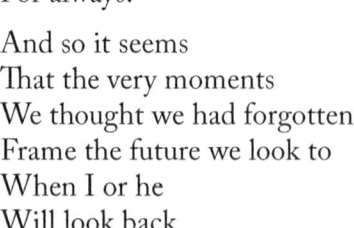

And so it seems
That the very moments
We thought we had forgotten
Frame the future we look to
When I or he
Will look back

Atop the hill
Climbed so many times before,
Feeling a new sensation
Like the mist creeping off the valley.
At that moment
Life seems what it is

And you,
A common face among many I know well enough,
And speaking a language you don't yet understand,
Reach my damaged faith
With the hidden mind
Which is your own.

Vision

All my life long
It seems
Your face has returned to me
Like a sea reforming itself
In a tide
Of half-remembered
Bits of laughter
And forgotten promise.

Our worlds
Are so often hidden
Or cloaked in music
Or movement
Seeking the eyes
That seem to agree.

The past is as mysterious
As any future
Which unfurls
Images yet to be grasped
Or possessed.
Harmony can't be searched for
Craved or Imagined.
It is already there
Inside us
Whatever we might think.

The Homecoming

An ocean of time
Divides Bell's sublime dream
From the well of its inspiration
And the inspiration of its creation,
Loved, revered
And captured in a flimsy frame
For all time
And for many, oblivious to the tides
Of History.

The gift of friendship
Linking forgotten ties
Of exploration and belonging,
Resumes its proper place
In the odd little town
That inspired Vancouver,
Seafarers, artists
And men of vision.

Our Dexter
Will welcome generations,
Who did not know or sense
His village of the imagination
And ancient nobility.

The Homecoming is about this painting by King's Lynn artist Walter Dexter being returned to its rightful place. But it's also about things coming full circle – just as I seem to have done.

His sense of Norfolk
And yellow church towers,
When they climb
Those venerable stairs
To the chamber
Built for the ambitious
And the curious.

That whirl of colour
Is one man's voice
And vision,
Of a town, Immortal in its
History and ways,
Loved like no other.
All Art and creation
Is born of longing and the search for home.
These mysterious things
Are what we are.

I Think I Caught a Glimpse of Heaven

The glare of the special suite
And Sister too
As she prowled
And lectured and cajoled
Encouragement, Was a curious curtain call
And greeting
To the years of memories
Waiting to be made
The endless promise
Of lives yet to be lived.
The rattling cups
And shoes that squeaked impatiently And shone
Under interrogators' lights
Jarred with the swirling feelings
Which had been waiting
Since before the beginning.

Clinical time seems endless
But not timeless,
My fears of laboratory conditions
And chemical smells
Which clean and burn
Like the pointless rules
Fierce, repeated and enforced
For my own good
They said.
I wanted to soar and leap
And sing my joy
At miracles
Beyond measure or control.

I remember telling the world my impatient news
Wetting the heads,

Recently my two eldest children completed the Three Peaks Challenge in appalling weather. Their strength and determination made me proud. Children often do.

Nothing prepares us for it. The hospital experience seems to have nothing to do with birth. Once I comforted a young father-to-be so nervous his cup and saucer rattled.

Nonetheless, when I think of the Queens Medical Centre in Nottingham, I smile at the way my children turned out.

Lightheaded, lightfooted
Changed forever
And exhilarated by exhaustion
And glimpses of imagined times
Memories already seen.
I sensed the smiles
To be exchanged,
The wisdom to learn
And to teach,
All rehearsed
Without knowing.

These fading thoughts
Are seen most clearly
Framed by limitless joy
And knowledge shared without speech
Or intent.
Gestures, movements, expressions
All unique and new
And yet somehow
Seen before.
I held my future in my arms
And saw my own past through other eyes.
I did not ask for this
But you set me free
And made me glad
That I lived.

In this poem I try to show that you have to feel at home with yourself, your history and where to live in order to be content.

No Hiding Place

Here it is always Winter
A place closed in
By stark stone walls
Where flint frost ground
Resists my feet
And any pretence of ease.
Steam of horses' breath
Mist and dark ,endless skies,
Gloomy tracks through ancient woods
Primeval, plaintive, terrible.
A world unprotected
Bitter beneath the huge moon
Reflecting the snow-covered fields.

Nearby the eternal sea
Blue, dead and dark
Or scurrying with horrible power
Past decaying wharves.
The salt is in our blood
The tides inspire the gulls
Which shriek tirelessly
At our complacency.
My tired brain
Is still cluttered
With dead thoughts.
Ruins and fragments
Lay forgotten
Dry, rasping, dull and derelict.
My thoughts are as heavy as my limbs
Riddled with some seeming disease.
Too far from stream, tree and leaf,
From the damp smelling breeze

And the lonely night time walks
Through the fields
Which brought me comfort
Then.

A distant echo of your laughter
Begins a new journey
A thin strain
Of your jaunty music
Seeps through my veins
And brings me back
To the place where joy and tears
Seem the same.

We have gazed across the frozen fields
Framing words forever
In the foggy grey,
Fresh and vital
Fused with the energy of the Sun
And the distant furrows
Which remember
And remind us
That we are all temporary
And only small.

In the familiar distance
Dark trees crouch dimly
Over barely liquid streams
Glowing in sluggish determination.
Such quiet joys as these,
Granted by a smile
Or a glance
Belie the simplicity of words
And fulfil all the hopes
Of our lost fathers.

The Endless River

To see the river's sky in dawning
The dark town in early morning
Still delights my searching mind,
Still brings sadness of a kind.
These brown banks
The ebb and flow
A lover's thanks
That only we can know.

The spirits of our friends
Walk beside us in this air
Pointing to a journey
Which we always sensed was there.

In the blink of an eye
Our time is nearly done,
The longing like shapes in a shifting sky
And the love of those we have known
Will always bring us here
Home.

Endpiece

What is a poem? At its most basic it's a sequence of words, so it's writing. But poetry is a form of human expression that has as much in common with music as writing.

A musical note is just a noise. Throw a bunch of them together at random and the discordant end result will sound like a troupe of monkeys playing hopscotch on a piano keyboard. But magic happens when a certain sequence of notes are played in the right order. Music at its most beautiful will move you to tears.

Likewise poetry, where words combined have a pleasing rhythm that stirs human emotions. Yet they're so much more than a pleasant melody because the words themselves are supercharged with a power that takes them deep into the human psyche. Poems can change the world – or at the very least enable you to look at the world and your own experiences and emotions in a different way.

Andrew Stephen's poems are invested with that power. But it's only now that this most reluctant of poets has decided to share them with the rest of the world.

This book has been a long time coming – more than half a century since a rebellious teenager first turned to verse to express his frustrations, loves and hopes.

The year was 1971. The joyous idealism of the Sixties had turned to the troubled uncertainly of a new decade and the young Andrew Stephen was trapped within the red-brick confines of a state boarding school, at war with the disciplinarian system and at odds with the rural backwater in which he found himself. He had no family to confide in; they were thousands of miles away in Cyprus, where his father was stationed with the RAF.

But he found he could express himself in poetry.

In the decades that followed, Andrew was able to turn the negativity of his authoritarian school years into a bright new style of education. As an English teacher in a succession of state secondary schools he helped inspire generations of young people to share his joy of the great poets. Meanwhile, his own early writings laid yellowing in a box and almost forgotten.

In the later years of his career, as a departmental head of English, Andrew got to inspire a new generation of teachers to – quite literally – spread the words of our great writers to yet more impressionable youngsters. Helping others to enjoy the beauty of literacy was his life's mission and he achieved it with aplomb.

You can read about Andrew's remarkable career in education in his best-selling memoir, *Reading, Writing & Redemption*, published in 2023 by The Hickathrift Press and available on Amazon, where it has deserved a succession of five-star reviews.

It is the remarkable autobiography of an extraordinary career – and it includes some extracts of Andrew's poetry. During the enforced isolation of the recent covid years Andrew had rekindled his love of writing poetry and was pleased enough with the end results to include a few lines of his verse to introduce the chapters of the book.

Those fragments of poetry were intriguing enough to earn the author some fulsome praise from his readers – and a clamour for more of the same. To cut a long story short, this book was published to satisfy that demand.

The original plan was Andrew and myself to collaborate and produce a book that showcased both Andrew's poetry and my own love of landscape photography, but it quickly became obvious that his powerful words created ample imagery of their own. Too many photographs of spectacular sunrises would distract from the potency of his poetry, so I've kept the images to a muted monochrome minimum. I hope you'll agree that they enhance the experience.

I love Andrew's stark, compelling poetry. Every word resonates and I find myself nodding my head in agreement at each shared experience. That he can weave so much imagery into so few words is the mark of a genius, but of course the great poets have been doing that since time immemorial.

Like Andrew, I'm a Norfolk lad with a love of words. In my case I've worked in the publishing industry all my adult life. The mission of the Hickathrift Press is to bring you great writing and powerful stories that would otherwise be untold. Expect many more in the near future.

Why The Hickathrift Press? It's named after one Thomas Hickathrift – a legendary giant whose outsize adventures took place at around the time of the Norman invasion. He roamed the treacherous undrained marshland of The Smeeth in west Norfolk, where he fought off evil ogres and looked after the downtrodden. It's where I'm from and I love that.

Stories told in verse predate literacy, so I suspect that Thomas Hickathrift himself would have appreciated Endless River. I hope you do, too.

(PS: If you enjoyed this book, please consider leaving an honest review on Amazon.)

Dave Phillips, Publisher
May 2024

More books from the Hickathrift Press

Reading, Writing & Redemption
By Andrew Stephen
If you enjoyed *Endless River* by Andrew Stephen you'll love his bestselling memoir *Reading, Writing & Redemption*, published in October 2023. This inspiring tale of his life in education reveals how, after a successful career as an English teacher, he returned as a governor to the very same school he had been wrongly expelled from as a teenager, half a century earlier.

It received rave 5-star reviews on Amazon, where it's available in paperback, hardback and Kindle formats. Go to: **https://shorturl.at/z8j8B**

The River Nene from Source to Sea
By David Phillips
Do you pronounce it Nen or Nene? And did you know that George Washington and the future King of Britain are related? You will learn this and much, much more besides as you join author David Phillips on a fascinating journey through history and along the lovely River Nene valley, meeting the ancestors of US presidents and other famous folk, as well as plenty of local heroes, along the way.

This is the definitive story of the River Nene and the settlements along its valley, from Northamptonshire, through Cambridgeshire to the sea in Lincolnshire.

No boater, angler or lover of the countryside and local history can afford to miss this book, which is available on Amazon in paperback and Kindle e-book formats. Go to: **https://shorturl.at/e3wxt**

How to Catch Pike
By David Phillips

Everything you need to know to catch big pike by lifelong pike angler Dave Phillips, in which he reveals the secrets of the pros - including location, weather conditions, tackle, tactics and bait. There are special sections on unhooking, handling and conservation, too.

All is explained in a no-nonsense style that's entertaining as well as easy to follow and packed with all the information you need to know to make you a better pike angler. By the time you've read this book you'll think like a pike.

You can order your copy on Amazon now in paperback or Kindle e-book format.
Go to: **https://shorturl.at/045sV**

Join the conversation . . .

Don't miss our interactive Facebook page!
You can catch all the latest news and updates on forthcoming book launches from The Hickathrift Press on our Facebook page. It's interactive, so readers and authors can join in the conversation.
Go to: **https://shorturl.at/50es3**

Hickathrift Press

Printed in Great Britain
by Amazon